presents

Notes to
Future Self

by Lucy Caldwell

First performed by Birmingham
Repertory Theatre Company at **mac**
in March 2011

Following the play's world premiere at
mac the production toured, supported
by the Sir Barry Jackson Trust

Birmingham Repertory Theatre
St George's Court
Albion Street
Birmingham
B1 3AH

birmingham-rep.co.uk

Notes to Future Self

by Lucy Caldwell

Philosophy Rainbow 'Sophie'
Imogen Doel

Daphne
Jane Lowe

Judy
Amanda Ryan

Peace Warrior Star Calliope 'Calliope'
Jayne Wisener

Director Rachel Kavanaugh

Designer Colin Richmond

Lighting Designer Simon Bond

Composer Catherine Jayes

Sound Designer Dan Hoole

Associate Director
Robert Shaw Cameron

Casting Director Alison Solomon

Dramaturg Caroline Jester

Stage Manager Paul Southern

Deputy Stage Manager
Sara Crathorne

Cast and Creative Team

Imogen Doel
Philosophy
Rainbow 'Sophie'

Training: LAMDA

Theatre credits include: *Get Santa!* (Royal Court).

Theatre credits while at drama school include: *Gas Station Angel Food, Tommy, The Revenger's Tragedy, The Grace of Mary Traverse, Nina, Three Sisters, The Man of Mode, A Midsummer Night's Dream, Oedipus Rex, 'Tis Pity She's A Whore.*

Television credits include: *An Accidental Farmer* (BBC).

Jane Lowe
Daphne

Theatre credits include: *Hedda Gabler* (West Yorkshire Playhouse); *True West* (Bristol Old Vic); *Long Time, No See* (Stratford Circus); *Venecia* (The Gate); *Lady Windermere's Fan* (Salisbury Playhouse); *My Mother Said I Never Should* (Oxford Stage Co/Young Vic); *The Verge* (Orange Tree); *Antigone/Little Creatures* (BAC); *Medea* (Wyndhams/ Broadway); *The Card* (Regent's Park); *Who's Afraid Of Virginia Woolf , Hay Fever, Steel Magnolias* (Ipswich); *Who's Afraid of..., Natural Causes* (Perth); *Rebecca* (Derby); *Rebecca* (Bromley); *Death of a Salesman* (Nottingham/ Farnham); *The Entertainer* (Farnham); *The Beaux Stratagem* (RSC); *Pack of Lies, Chez Nous* (Watermill); *Waving* (Monstrous Regiment); *To Kill a Mocking Bird, Me Mam Sez, A Man for All Seasons* (Nottingham); *Camille* (Leeds); *Tristram Shandy* (Oxford); *Mandragola* (National); *Death of a Salesman* (Manchester); *Deathtrap* (Tour); *The Best Man, Cabaret, Saturday Sunday Monday* (Edinburgh); *Bodies, Filumena, Present Laughter, Maintenance Man, Norman Conquests, Macbeth, Saturday Sunday Monday, Cabaret* (Liverpool); *Old Times* (Ipswich); *The Price* (Basingstoke); *Barefoot in the Park* (Haymarket).

Television credits include: *Moving On II: Losing My Religion, Doctors, Hustle, Holby City, Silent Witness, Judge John Deed, Crime and Punishment, Down to Earth, EastEnders, Casualty, Next of Kin, Lovejoy, Sam's Duck, Gallow Glass, Tales From Hollywood, Tygo Road, Johnny Briggs, One By One, Late Starter, I Woke Up One Morning, Cockles, The Strange Affair of Adelaide Harris, Telford's Change, Spend, Spend, Spend, Daft As a Brush, Wednesday Love* (BBC); *The Bill, The Royal, Housewife 49* (ITV); *Spooks* (Kudos); *Cold Blood I + II, Wokenwell, Cracker, The Practice, Young Sherlock, Lady Killers, Life for Christine, Leave it to Charlie, The Nearly Man* (Granada); *Heartbeat* (YTV); *Bad Girls (Two Series)* (LWT); *Four Fathers, Blonde Bombshell, Peak Practice* (Carlton); *Samson Super-Slug* (Red Rooster); *May To December* (Cinema Verity); *Bye Bye Baby* (Harbour); *Shrinks* (Euston); *Perfect Scoundrels* (TVS); *Boon* (Central); *Hands, Rooms* (Thames); *Casting The Runes* (Yorkshire) and *Westway* (Harlech).

Film credits include: *Seven Lives*

Radio credits include: Many plays for BBC Manchester and London

Amanda Ryan
Judy

Trained: Royal Academy of Dramatic Art

Theatre credits include: *Shrunk* (Cock Tavern Theatre); *A Winter's Tale* (Headlong); *Wuthering Heights* (Birmingham Repertory Theatre/Tour); *Otherwise Engaged* (Criterion); *A Streetcar Named Desire* (Theatre Clwyd); *Closer* (National Theatre Tour) and *The Wood Demon* (Playhouse Theatre).

Television credits include: *Lewis - Wild Justice* (ITV); *Shameless* - Series 4, 5 & 6 (Company Prod); *Midsomer Murders* (Bentley Productions); *EastEnders* (BBC); *The Amazing Mrs Pritchard* (Kudos); *Christmas Merry* (Calling the Shots); MIT (Talkback Thames); (BBC); *Dalziel and Pascoe* (BBC); *The Inspector Lynley Mysteries* (BBC); *A Great Deliverance* (BBC); *Attachments* - 2 series (World Prods); *David Copperfield* (BBC); *Kavanagh QC* (Carlton); *Supply & Demand* (La Plante Prods.);*The Hunger* (RSA/ Showtime); *The Swords* (RSA/Showtime); *Inspector Morse* (Zenith/Carlton); *The New Adventures Of Robin Hood* (Warner Brothers); *Wycliffe* (HTV); *Poldark* (pilot) (HTV).

Film credits include: *Sparkle* (Magic Light Pics); *Red Mercury* (Inspired Movies); *Whoosh* (Sweet Child Films); *Stealing Lives* (Stone City Films); *Best* (Best Films Ltd); *Britannic* (Regent Productions); *The Escort* (Pathe Productions); *Simon Magus* (Silesia Films); *Elizabeth I* (Working Title); *The Man Who Held His Breath* (Miracle Films); *Metroland* (Blue Horizon); *Woodlanders* (River Films); *Jude* (Obscure Films).

Jayne Wisener
Peace Warrior Star
Calliope 'Calliope'

Theatre credits include: *Parade* (Donmar Warehouse); *The Secret Garden* (West Yorkshire Playhouse); *West Side Story, My Fair Lady, Oklahoma!* and *Jesus Christ Superstar* (all for Music Theatre 4 Youth).

Television credits include: *Vexed, The Inbetweeners, Casualty, Minder,* the upcoming *Injustice* and *The Runaway*

Film credits include: *Life Just Is, Jane Eyre, Boogeyman III, A Kiss For Jed Wood* and *Sweeney Todd: The Demon Barber Of Fleet Street* in which she starred opposite Johnny Depp, Alan Rickman, Helena Bonham Carter and Sacha Baron Cohen.

Jayne can also be seen playing both a young girl and her evil doppelganger in the band Archive's 2009 music video for their single '*Bullets*'.

Lucy Caldwell
Writer

Lucy Caldwell's plays include *Leaves* and *Guardians* and her radio dramas include *Girl from Mars* and *Avenues of Eternal Peace*. Her plays have won several awards, including the George Devine Award, the Susan Smith Blackburn Prize, the BBC Stewart Parker Award, the Imison Award, and the PMA Award for Most Promising Playwright. Lucy is also a critically acclaimed novelist, author of *Where They Were Missed* and *The Meeting Point*.

Rachel Kavanaugh
Director

Rachel is Artistic Director of Birmingham Repertory Theatre, where credits include: *The Cherry Orchard, Arthur And George, His Dark Materials, Hapgood, Peter Pan - A Musical Adventure, Uncle Vanya, Martha, Josie And The Chinese Elvis, The Wizard Of Oz, Racing Demon, Murmuring Judges, The Absence Of War* and *The Lady In The Van.* Also *A Doll's House* (Birmingham Repertory Theatre/UK tour); *The Madness Of George III* (with West Yorkshire Playhouse) and *Arcadia* (with Bristol Old Vic).

Other theatre credits include: *Love Story* (Minerva Studio, Chichester and West End); *The Music Man* and *A Small Family Business* (Chichester Festival Theatre); *Hilda* (Hampstead Theatre); *The Rivals* (Bristol Old Vic); *Dracula* (UK tour); *The Merry Wives Of Windsor* and *Alice In Wonderland* (RSC); *The Taming Of The Shrew, Cymbeline, The Two Gentlemen Of Verona, As You Like It, Love's Labour's Lost, Much Ado About Nothing, Twelfth Night* and *A Midsummer Night's Dream* (Open Air Theatre, Regent's Park); *Romeo And Juliet* (Washington Shakespeare Theatre); *Guys And Dolls* (Sheffield Crucible); *A View From The Bridge* (Greenwich Theatre); *Eva Peron, The Walls* and *Saigon Rose* (Orange Tree Theatre).

Colin Richmond
Designer

Trained at the Royal Welsh College of music and Drama, Cardiff. First Class BA Hons. Lord Williams Design Award 2002 and 2003.

2003 Linbury Prize Finalist and a Resident Designer as part of the Royal Shakespeare Company's Trainee Programme 2004-2005.

Colin's credits include: *Entertaining Mr Sloane, Touched* for the very first time, *Ring Round The Moon, Bad Girls-The Musical, The RSC production of Breakfast With Mugabe* (West End) Notes to Future Self, The Cherry Orchard, *A Christmas Carol, Hapgood, The Bolt Hole, 'Lowdat* (Birmingham Rep Theatre), *Twelfth Night, Bad Girls – The Musical, Bollywood Jane, Salonika, Hapgood, Animal Farm, Billy Liar, A Christmas Carol* (West Yorkshire Playhouse), *L'Opera Seria (Italy), Hansel and Gretel* (Northampton Theatre Royal),

Play/Not I (BAC), *Human Rites* (Old Southwark Playhouse), *House Of The Gods!, Letters of a Love Betrayed* (MTW/ Royal Opera House 2/ National Tour), *Restoration* (Bristol Old Vic, Headlong Theatre), The *Shadow Of A Gunman* (Glasgow Citizens), *Hansel & Gretel,* Sondheim's *Sweeney Todd* (TMA Best Musical Production 2010), *The Firebird* (Dundee Rep Theatre), *Suddenly Last Summer* (Theatr Clwyd), *Europe* (Barbican), *Absent Friends* (Oldham Coliseum), *The May Queen* (Liverpool Everyman), *Amadeus* (The Crucible, Sheffield), *All the Fun of The Fair* (Number 1 National Tour), *When We Are Married* (West Yorkshire Playhouse/Liverpool Playhouse), *La Boheme, Don Pasquale* (Opera Holland Park, Kensington), *The Lady in the Van* (Salisbury Playhouse), *The Caucasian Chalk Circle* (Shared Experience/WYP/ Nottingham Playhouse), *The Three Musketeers* and *The Princess of Spain* (English Touring Theatre/ Traverse/ Coventry), *Great Expectations* (Watford Palace Theatre, English Touring Theatre).

Television credits include: First series and pre-production assistant designer on *Doctor Who* (BBC Wales).

Simon Bond
Lighting Designer

Simon is a Lighting Technician at Birmingham Repertory Theatre.

Recent designs include: *Respect, Cling To Me Like Ivy, 8sixteen32* and *Looking For Yoghurt.*

Catherine Jayes
Composer

As Musical Director/Arranger: *Oklahoma!* (Chichester Festival Theatre); *Animal Farm* (West Yorkshire Playhouse); *Guys And Dolls, Sweet Charity* (Sheffield Crucible); *Amadeus* (Wilton's Music Hall); *High Society, Gypsy, Fiddler On The Roof, The Messiah* (West Yorkshire Playhouse); *Merrily We Roll Along, Irma La Douce, Carmen* (the Watermill, Newbury); *Candide* (Liverpool Everyman, where she was an associate director).

Catherine was Music Director at the Open Air Theatre, Regent's Park for many years. Shows included: *The Pirates Of Penzance; Kiss Me, Kate; Camelot* and *The Boy Friend.*

As Composer: *The Cherry Orchard, His Dark Materials, Hapgood, Uncle Vanya* (Birmingham Repertory Theatre); *Macbeth, Cymbeline, The Duchess Of Malfi, Troilus And Cressida* (Cheek by Jowl); *The Mandate* (National Theatre); *Arcadia* (Bristol Old Vic); *The Letter* (Wyndhams); *Great Expectations* (Royal Shakespeare Company); *A Midsummer Night's Dream, The Merry Wives Of Windsor, Henry IV* Part 2 and many more at the Open Air.

Films include: *Charlie And The Chocolate Factory, De-lovely* and *Sweeney Todd.*

Catherine is an associate director of Cheek by Jowl.

Dan Hoole
Sound Designer

Dan is Head of Sound at Birmingham Repertory Theatre.

Robert Shaw Cameron
Associate Director

Robert is Resident Associate Director at The REP; he trained at Webber Douglas Academy of Dramatic Art and the University of Birmingham.

He has worked as both director and actor in theatre and television. As Director: *First Person Shooter, Just So, Grass Routes: Cuttings* (Birmingham Repertory Theatre); *White Open Spaces* (Soho Theatre/UK tour/National Theatre of Sweden); *A Florentine Tragedy* (Florence); *1.60.3600* (Regent Park Studio/Young Vic); *Love at First* (Edinburgh); *Road, Guys and Dolls, Blood Wedding, Queen Coal, The Crucible* (University of Cumbria); *The Ribbon Cage* (RADA).

As Assistant Director: *A Christmas Carol* (West Yorkshire Playhouse); *Arthur & George, Respect* (Birmingham Repertory Theatre); *The Taming of the Shrew, A Midsummer Night's Dream, The Boyfriend* (Regent's Park); *The Castle Spectre.*

As an actor, theatre work includes: *Smoke, As You Like It* (New Vic); *Dracula, Precious Bane, Death of a Salesman, A Christmas Carol* (UK tours). Television and film work includes: *The Bill, The Wild Life, Shane, Where the Heart Is, The Basil Brush Show, EastEnders, Holby City, Heartbeat, Keen Eddie* and the feature film *Ibsen's Ghosts.*

Alison Solomon
Casting Director

As Casting Director for Birmingham Repertory Theatre: *Respect, Behna (Sisters), The Wiz (Community Cast), Grass Routes Festival, East is East* with Sooki McShane as lead Casting Director, *These Four Streets, Looking For Yoghurt* British cast (Birmingham Repertory Theatre, Joyful Theatre and kijimuna Festa in association with Hanyong Theatre); *Rosetta Life, Toy Theatres, The Speckled Monster* (Birmingham Repertory Theatre in Association with University of Birmingham); *At The Gates of Gaza* – UK Writers Guild Award for best play 2009 (Big Creative Ideas in Association with Birmingham Repertory Theatre); *360 Degrees (GENERATION), TRANSMISSIONS Festival 'The Big 10'.*

Norman Beaton Fellowship 2011, 2010 & 2008 - BBC Radio Drama (Birmingham) and Birmingham Repertory Theatre.

As Children's Casting Director for Birmingham Repertory Theatre: *A Christmas Carol, The Grapes of Wrath, Orphans, Once On This Island, An Inspector Calls, Hapgood, Peter Pan, Wizard of Oz, Galileo.*

Recent workshops / readings include: *Gravity, Shell Shock, Bookface, Mustafa, Transmissions, Without Parade, Our House, Crimescene, Revolution By Reason, Upload, ID-79, Pwnage, Broken Stones, Notes to Future Self, Grass Routes Workshops, Coming Out from the Cold, Fairytale Toy Theatres, Dealing With Dreams, Bazaar, Cling to Me Like Ivy, Respect, Dirty Fingernails; Uncle Mustafa's Djinn, Dido, The Mezzanine, After the Accident, Loosing the Race.*

Alison is delighted to have worked as Casting Director on *Notes to Future Self* with such wonderful people as Rachel Kavanaugh, Lucy Caldwell and Robert Shaw Cameron and our wonderful actors.

Caroline Jester
Dramaturg

Caroline is Dramaturg at Birmingham Repertory Theatre and has taught on the MPhil in Playwriting at Birmingham University and various undergraduate programmes. She is the co-author of *Playwriting Across the Curriculum,* published by Routledge, and has worked as a freelance dramaturg, director and workshop leader.

Birmingham Repertory Theatre Company

THE REP | A CHANGE OF SCENERY

Birmingham Repertory Theatre

Birmingham Repertory Theatre is one of Britain's leading national producing theatre companies.

The REP's first ever off-site programme gets under way in 2011 as the company begins its two-year adventure performing at different venues across Birmingham. This 'Change of Scenery' comes as a result of The REP's integration with the new Library of Birmingham currently under construction and due for completion in 2013.

The REP's Artistic Director Rachel Kavanaugh has programmed a varied season of work for 2011 including the world premiere of Lucy Caldwell's *Notes To Future Self*, a co-production of *The Wiz* with West Yorkshire Playhouse plus a return to the company's repertory roots with a pairing of two plays, *The Importance Of Being Earnest* and *Travesties* in repertoire at the company's original home – The Old Rep.

The commissioning and production of new work lies at the core of The REP's programme. Developing new and particularly younger audiences is also at the heart of The REP's work. The theatre's Learning and Participation department engage with over 10,000 young people each year through various initiatives including The Young REP, REP's Children, Grass Routes writing programme for 18–30 year olds and the Transmissions Playwriting in schools programme.

The REP's productions regularly transfer to London and tour nationally and internationally. Tours during 2009 included a new staging of Philip Pullman's *His Dark Materials*, Dennis Kelly's *Orphans*, Simon Stephens' *Pornography*, Charlie Dark's *Have Box Will Travel*, *Looking For Yoghurt* – a new play for young children which played at theatres in the UK, Japan and Korea – and *These Four Streets*, a multi-authored play inspired by the 2005 Lozells disturbances.

2011–2013 will be a significant period of development in the history of Birmingham Repertory Theatre as it integrates with the new £193 million Library of Birmingham, which will be built adjacent to the theatre. This development opportunity will allow the theatre to make many improvements to its current building as well as sharing a new 300-seat flexible studio theatre with the Library of Birmingham. The period will also bring an exciting time artistically as audiences will be able to enjoy and experience an imaginative programme of REP productions in other theatres and non-theatrical spaces across Birmingham. The theatre is due to reopen in 2013, a fitting celebration for The REP's Centenary year.

Artistic Director **Rachel Kavanaugh**
Executive Director **Stuart Rogers**

Box Office: 0121 236 4455
Administration: 0121 245 2000
birmingham-rep.co.uk

Birmingham Repertory Theatre is a registered charity, number 223660

Lucy Caldwell
Notes to Future Self

for John & Pam,
with love,
Lucy x

faber and faber

First published in 2011
by Faber and Faber Limited
74–77 Great Russell Street, London WC1B 3DA

Typeset by Country Setting, Kingsdown, Kent CT14 8ES
Printed in England by CPI Bookmarque, Croydon, Surrey

A CIP record for this book
is available from the British Library

ISBN 978-0-571-27724-7

2 4 6 8 10 9 7 5 3 1

For Kim
(and poor Louisa on the wagon trail)

Acknowledgements

I would like to thank Rachel Kavanaugh and Caroline Jester and everyone else at Birmingham Rep, who have been so supportive during the writing of this play. Also Harriet, for her boundless patience and cheerleading, and Natalie, who read draft after draft. Steve and Dinah at Faber, and Simon Trussler, for their work on this text. Thank you Jo and Vaughan, my Midlands home from home. Thank you Dr Kim Caldwell, to whom this play is dedicated, and of whom I'm so proud. And most of all, thank you to Nina, and to Nadia, who gave me the soul and the spark of this play. I'll raise a Sidecar to you.

This play was completed with the help of a grant from the Peggy Ramsay Foundation. I am very grateful for the Foundation's generosity, which gave me such precious space and time to write.

Author's Notes

This play is written to be done with a minimal set – the less there is, the better. We see Sophie (as she explains a little into the play) as she sees herself, not as others see her. This can be accentuated with costume; while the other characters can be dressed literally or representationally (Daphne in a skirt and blouse, Judy in a long hippy skirt or Thai fishermen's pants, Calliope in school uniform or jeans) and remain the same throughout, Sophie can change costumes according to her mood – a strapless scarlet ball dress with peacock feathers in her hair, for example, is more in keeping with the spirit of the play than pyjamas or sick-room garb.

Characters

Philosophy Rainbow ('Sophie')
thirteen

Peace Warrior Star Calliope ('Calliope')
her sister, sixteen

Judy
thirty-four, their mother

Daphne
sixty, Judy's mother

NOTES TO FUTURE SELF

Time

Present day. Early autumn to early winter.

The time is centred around Sophie. All other characters are at the mercy of her time's swirls and eddies.

Place

Sophie's world. Her fears, desires, consolations, memories, hopes.

There are also a handful of 'literal' scenes. The 'literal' setting is Daphne's house, a small two-bedroomed terrace in Kings Heath, Birmingham. The house has a small garden with a shed, and overlooks a communal area with a small, basic children's playground: slide, swings, see-saw. This is the view from Sophie's bedroom.

ONE

*Sophie is at the centre of the stage. The others are in
'their' spaces, separate pools of light around her. Daphne
in the 'kitchen', making a shopping list. Judy in the
'shed', meditating. Calliope in the 'attic', going through
photographs. They are not frozen, but neither are they
moving in real time, quite.*

Sophie There was once a boy born in rural India who
grew up insisting he was someone else.

This is a true story.

As soon as he could talk he said to the woman who'd
given birth to him, 'You're not my mother, and he's not
my father and –' get this, 'Where is my wife and where
are my babies?' At first they laughed. Then they dismissed
it. Then they got angry. But no matter what they did, the
little boy kept on. 'Why call me this name, it isn't my name.
Why live in this house, it isn't my house. Where is my
wife and where are my babies and when can I see them?'

One day, a documentary maker arrived from America,
researching – (*slightly awkward*) 'Paths to Enlightenment'.
And he heard about the boy, who was eight or nine by now,
and went to visit the family, taking a translator with him
because this is a little village in the back end of nowhere.
And through the translator the most fantastical story
emerged. The little boy spoke about his wife, and their
children, and their house, in a village of mangroves and
coconut trees by the sea. And the American's documentary
wasn't going very well, so he thought: why the hell not?

So they all pile in his jeep and go in search of this
village. And it takes them four days and nights to get
there – this is further than the little boy has ever travelled

in his life. But when they get to the village, it is exactly as he'd described. I mean *exactly*. And his eyes shine and his face flushes and he directs them through the dirt tracks, and when the tracks run out he jumps from the jeep and runs, and he runs so fast they almost lose him. And they follow him through the mangroves to a small concrete house where a woman in a red sari is washing clothes, and the little boy yells her name, and man does she get a fright, turning around to see this entourage of people, camera crew and everything.

And no one knows what to do when the boy says, 'This is my wife, and this is our house.' And he knows where everything is, he goes round the rooms saying, 'Where's the television gone? Why have you moved this? What happened to my bicycle?' And then he says, 'Where are my children?' And the woman says, 'My children are out playing,' and the boy runs outside to a clearing where sure enough a gaggle of village kids are kicking a football, and without hesitating he goes over and calls two of them by name, both boys, both older than him.

And no one knows what to do, because this is getting seriously weird. But the camera keeps rolling, and there's all these people there by then, shouting and yelling, and the translator's translating so fast he's gabbling and sweating, and it turns out –

Right –

It turns out –

That the woman's husband had died suddenly, exactly nine months before the boy was born, cycling home from work one evening, a rifle shot that wasn't meant to be for him. And when they shaved the boy's head they found a mark, like a bullet wound, in exactly the place it should be.

If you don't believe me you can see for yourself, it's all on film and anyone can watch it, you can get it on Amazon or anywhere.

14

And there's loads more I haven't told you, like how the little boy tells the woman all sorts of private things he shouldn't be able to know, like how they made love and where their children were conceived and what they argued about and the pet names they had for each other and stuff.

(*Slightly self-consciously.*) You see, normally we don't remember anything about our past lives, only in dreams and fragments, like if you're irrationally frightened of water maybe you died once by drowning. But because this man's death was so sudden and so violent, and because that wasn't when he was meant to die, his memories had survived intact, and he'd come back to earth in search of his former life.

My name is Philosophy Rainbow and these are the last weeks of my life. It's Monday the seventh of September and by the time you see this I won't be here any more.

We could go on for ages about the meaning of 'I' and the meaning of 'here'. Believe me, I know. It's all Judy ever does.

She nods to Judy.

Judy's my mom. It's an understatement to say she's a bit of a hippy. You might have guessed that from her name. I mean, who else but a New Ager calls their baby 'Philosophy Rainbow'?

I try to go by 'Sophie'. I'd like you to think of me as 'Sophie', no matter what anyone else might call me. And no matter how many times Judy snorts and goes – (*high-pitched sing-song*) 'Sit on the sofa, Sophie,' as if it's a boring, bourgeois, *comfy* name.

Mind you, I got off lightly compared to my sister.

She nods to Calliope.

Her name is Peace Warrior Star Calliope. There's not much you can do with that.

I'll introduce you to them properly, Judy and Calliope, so you know who they are. And Daphne, whose house this is. We came here at Easter, when I was first diagnosed. Before that we lived in – (*she takes a breath and reels them off*) San Francisco – Ocala Forest – Washington DC – Goa – Kerala – Findhorn, Scotland – Cornwall – the warehouse in London – the minivan in Europe – Almeria, Spain – Morocco. That was where I got sick, Morocco, and we came back to Birmingham, cos Judy didn't know where else to go or where to get medical care. I'm only thirteen but you could say I've led a very full and varied life. Judy says that. She says whenever people judge Calliope or me we are to look them straight in the eye and say to ourselves: 'I have been more places and seen more things than the limitations of your world will even allow for.'

She really doesn't get it.

She nods to Daphne.

Daphne is Judy's mother, our grandmother. We'd never met her before we turned up at Easter on her doorstep. Well, apart from when we were babies, and that doesn't count because we don't remember. Imagine that. You don't see your daughter or grandchildren for twelve and a half years, then one day you answer a knock on the door and there they all are on the doorstep. 'Hi, Gran, long time no see, we're your long-lost family and we're coming to live with you or rather should we say *die* with you. Oh yes, sorry, did we not mention, Sophie here is about to be diagnosed with terminal bone cancer and by the time they catch it it'll've spread to her central nervous system and be too late to do much really. But the up side is we won't be here too long. Surprise!'

She watches Daphne. Daphne sighs and frowns over her list.

Judy always talked of Daphne like she was a wicked old hag but when we actually met her she was just a nice, normal middle-aged lady with a skirt and blouse and salt-and-pepper hair.

Well, this is Daphne's house. It's a two-bedroom terrace in Kings Heath, on the outskirts of Birmingham. It's perfectly nice, neat, normal – unexceptional in every way. It's hard to believe that a house like this produced someone like Judy.

Or maybe this house is exactly why she's the way she is.

This is the back bedroom, that used to be hers. Big heavy wardrobe, smelling of mothballs, chest of drawers, smelling of lavender sachets. Single bed and window overlooking the common, with a children's play area: battered metal slide, see-saw, couple of swings, you know the sort.

Judy and Calliope sleep in the front room, Cal on an air mattress and Judy on the couch. This house wasn't built for a family. Two bedrooms, one bathroom, front room, kitchen-diner. Handkerchief lawn and garden shed, bricked enclosure for the bins. Oh, and attic. Calliope spends a lot of her time in the attic. She thinks nobody notices or knows where she is.

Sophie moves into Calliope's space. Calliope is poring over a handful of photographs.

Cal is obsessed with finding out who her father is. Since we got here, and she found the photos in the attic, she's hatching a plan to go to Greece and track him down. All we know is that his name is Nikos and he was a waiter in the Blue Sky Café. It was her first holiday abroad, and her first time away from home. She was seventeen and he said he loved her. When she went back at Christmas, he pretended he didn't know who she was.

Calliope Look how young they look.

Sophie She looks younger than you.

Calliope And pretty. She looks . . . happy.

Calliope goes through the photos again.

Sophie She was all set to go to art school, and her parents were disapproving enough of that as it was. So . . .

Faintly, the soundtrack of The Beatles, 'She's Leaving Home'.

She left.

I always imagine it to that soundtrack, even though that's silly, really, because it was released a decade before Judy was even born. When she left home, the songs topping the charts were –

Calliope is now going through a box of CD singles.

Whitney Houston, 'I Will Always Love You', 'Can't Help Falling in Love' by UB40 and 'Whoomp! There It Is' by the Tag Team.

Judy, your taste in music was terrible.

Calliope giggles, stuffs the CDs back in the box. Then takes out another one, slowly turns it round in her hands.

Ugly Kid Joe, 'Cat's in the Cradle'. She loved that song. She always used to sing it to Calliope.

Calliope sings the first verse of 'Cat's in the Cradle'.
Sophie moves away and the scene with Calliope fades a bit. Sophie moves towards Judy's space.

She fell in with some New Agers, loads of them were artists and art school dropouts and out-of-work actors and musicians, and they used to travel all about the countryside with sound systems putting on raves. It wasn't like you'd think. It was really friendly, at the start. They shared food and slept in minivans or yurts and loads of them brought their babies and children with them.

Judy is sitting cross-legged in the junk and debris of the garden shed, trying to meditate.

When it started to fall apart, as all things eventually do, she got to hearing of this place in California, where a bunch of people who called themselves the Rainbow People lived in the redwood forest in peace and harmony. You've probably guessed, that's where I was born.

Sophie watches Judy for a moment.

She's thinking about that, now. She's thinking about when I was born, and where, and how it came to this.

Judy sighs. She looks very sad.

(*Impulsively, as a child.*) Tell me about my dad, Judy.

Judy (*as if addressing a small child in front of her*) Your dad was the kindest, gentlest, most loveliest of boys . . . (*She trails off.*)

Sophie (*prompting*) He used to sit and drum all night . . .

Judy He used to sit and drum all night and after a while it was like he *was* the heartbeat of the forest. He reminded me of a young god, you know, one of the boy-gods from the legends, smooth-limbed and curly-haired. I always wonder what happened to him.

Sophie (*softly*) What do you think did happen?

Judy I don't know . . . I wish he'd stayed with me. I would have followed him anywhere . . . But he was a true free spirit, you know, too free to stay with anyone, anywhere, for very long.

(*Remembering saying this.*) And if I've tried to teach you one thing, Philosophy, just one thing, it's that you can't and shouldn't own people. That's what relationships are,

19

or what they inevitably become. Think of how we talk about other people: *my* boyfriend, *my* husband, *my* mother, *my* daughter. We use the possessive, it's right there, built into the very heart of the way we designate a relationship. (*Coming into the present, trying to convince herself now, the little child forgotten.*) And therein lies the cause of so much unhappiness. You are your own person, just as I am my own, and Calliope, and Daphne, and anyone else. You are your own and nobody else's, and nobody else is yours. And once you realise that, and when you practise it, only then will you be free, or at least a little freer.

> *Pause.*
> *Judy's words sound so hollow. She takes out a tin and starts to roll a spliff.*

Sophie (*gently*) Judy, you promised.

Judy I promised I'd *try*!

Sophie Well, then you're not trying very hard.

Judy You can't even begin to imagine how hard it is for me. Being back here . . . in my mother's house . . . while my child –
My child –

> *Judy begins to weep, silently, her head in her hands. Sophie watches. Judy weeps.*

Sophie Remember your mantra, Judy.

Judy I can't do it. It's no use. I don't know what to do. I can't do it.

Sophie Don't get flustered. Don't give up. You mustn't give up.

Judy I'm trying my hardest and I just can't do it, I can't subdue my mind, I'm trying to tell myself to, to, to acknowledge the thoughts and let them pass but I just can't do it. I should take off, slip away, you'll all be better off without me.

Sophie Do your deep breathing, OK? Come on, I'll do it with you. In for a count of six . . .

Judy closes her eyes and starts to breathe. Then her eyes snap open.

Judy It's no use.

Sophie Come on.

Judy I can't concentrate in here. I can't get beyond myself. I need light, and air. I need –

Sophie Light some incense. That'll help. Some sandalwood. You've always liked sandalwood best.

Judy finds a stick of incense and lights it.

That's better. Isn't that better? Now. Try your healing mantra.

Judy sighs, recrosses her legs and closes her eyes.

Judy Picture twenty thousand people in a sunlit meadow, standing silent in prayer, holding hands in a huge, unbroken circle. Picture the silence growing slowly into a thrum of voices united in a single '*om*' reverberating through the valley and into the hills beyond. Hold the '*om*' in your mind. Let it spread through you and around you and in you. Picture twenty thousand people in a sunlit meadow . . . *etc.*

As Judy is repeating her mantra, the scene fades again, and Sophie moves towards Daphne in the kitchen.

Sophie Daphne's planning what meals we'll eat this week and trying to work out how her pension will stretch to them. Judy's got dole money and they've got an allowance for me but it doesn't go very far.

Daphne Bread, milk, Crunchy-Nut Cornflakes.

Sophie They're expensive, but she's got a soft spot for Calliope.

Daphne Sausages, onion. Beans, eggs. Cheddar, tomatoes, mince. Apples. Chicken stock for soup for Sophie.

A wall clock chimes five o'clock.

Sophie Five o'clock already. You'd better get dinner on, Daphne, so you're in time for your prayer group.

They've been praying for me every Monday for the past two months. I wish I believed in prayer. I wish I believed in God, too. It'd be nice, the thought of God and his angels and all the fluffy clouds and choirs waiting for me.

Daphne says that God's calling me back to him.

It doesn't feel like he's calling me so much as a nightmare game of hide-and-seek. Fee-fi-fo-fum, where are you, Sophie? I'm coming to get you . . . You can run but you can't hide.

(*Suddenly, vehemently.*) I hate your God, Daphne! I don't even believe in him but I hate him, anyway!

Daphne stands up abruptly.

Daphne Right. (*She opens a cupboard, looks in. Sighs. Decides.*) Boiled eggs and toast it'll be. (*Calls.*) Judy?

No answer.

Calliope?

Calliope enters, breathless and shifty.

Calliope I was doing my homework upstairs.

Sophie Liar. She's not stupid, Calliope.

Daphne Seen your mum?

22

Calliope Judy's in the shed.

They share a moment. Daphne rolls her eyes.

Daphne And Sophie's still sleeping?

Calliope I think so.

Daphne After tea, will you take her up her vitamin pills?

Calliope Vitamin C, Vitamin E, Vitamin A. Selenium –

Sophie To help the body absorb Vitamin E.

Calliope Zinc –

Daphne To help with the Vitamin C.

Calliope Copper –

Sophie To make sure the zinc doesn't overbalance my potassium.

Calliope Mega-dose of B vitamins –

Sophie *and* **Daphne** And Brewer's Yeast to help.

Calliope Astragalus –

Sophie For boosting energy and fighting fatigue.

Calliope Royal jelly –

Daphne To halt the growth of stomach bacteria.

Calliope Bee pollen –

Sophie To fight chronic infections.

Calliope Echinacea –

Daphne To help move lymph.

Calliope Siberian ginseng –

Sophie *and* **Daphne** To help with stress.

Calliope And wild blue-green algae.

Daphne Which contains practically every nutrient, vitamin, mineral, amino acid and live enzyme known to man.

Sophie And which tastes – I'm not kidding – like liquid green diarrhoea.

Daphne Poor little love.

Sophie Half of Daphne's pension goes on vitamins and supplements. For all the good they do, I may as well scrunch up the money and eat it myself. But she insists.

Daphne God love her. God love us all.
   Right, Calliope. I'm going to do us a boiled egg for tea tonight.

Calliope OK. But I'm not really hungry.

Daphne You have to eat something, keep your strength up. (*She looks at her.*) Was it school today?

Calliope No.

Daphne Are you really settling in OK?

Calliope Yeah.

Daphne looks at her. Suddenly, vehemently:

Daphne It's none of my business, I'm sure, but what your mother put the two of you through –

Calliope I'm not actually that behind. I'm better than any of the others at languages.

Daphne Languages! Maths and Physics and, and History and the rest of it is what you need. And forget subjects, you need friends. Have you made any friends yet?

Calliope (*burst*) Friends? They think I'm weird, Daphne. I don't know the right music, I don't know TV

24

programmes. They talk about stuff and I haven't a clue what they're talking about.

Daphne Oh, love. It'll get better. It's only been a week.

Calliope (*clams up*) Yeah.

Daphne You'll make friends.

Calliope (*quietly*) How can I? I can hardly bring them back here anyway, can I?

Daphne Beg pardon?

Calliope Nothing.

A moment.

Daphne Lay the table, now, will you.

Calliope sets about laying the table for three. (There needn't be literal props.)

I'll take this to your sister. (*A tray of toast and a boiled egg.*)

Daphne leaves with the tray. Calliope lays the table. Sophie watches. Daphne leaves the tray in Sophie's bedroom. As she stands and turns, Judy stands, too. They come into the kitchen together, and sit down with Calliope, in unison.

Now.
Judy, will you say grace?

Judy Mom . . .

Daphne (*briskly*) Yes, Judy.

Judy How many times . . .

Daphne We're in my house now, Judy, my house. My house, my rules. Now please say grace.

Judy stares at Daphne.

Calliope Just say it, Judy.

Daphne wins.

Judy (*as sarcastically as she dares*)
Some hae meat and cannae eat
And some wad eat that want it
But we hae meat and we can eat
And so the Laird be thankit.

*Daphne glares at her. Judy does not meet her eye.
A moment. Judy wins.*

Daphne (*curtly*) Amen.

*They eat. Sophie watches. The only dialogue is the
following.*

Daphne Pass the salt please, Calliope.

Calliope Pass the butter, Judy?

Judy The pepper?

Sophie Happy days in the Cunningham household.

The scene fades a bit, or slows.

I have this dream. This nightmare. I'm outside a house
looking in, and inside it's Christmas, and the people
inside are decorating the tree and hanging stockings and
listening to carols and laughing. And there's a fire
burning and it all looks so cosy, and outside where I am
it's starting to snow. And they come to the window to
look at the snow, but they don't see me there, and I
knock at the window, I knock and knock but they don't
see me, they just look right through me. And then I start
to bang the window and I bang so hard I think the glass
must break, but it doesn't, and still they don't hear me.
And then one of them comes over and draws the curtains
and I can't see any more and I know that I am dead and
this is death.

She has got increasingly worked up during the above.
She is circling them in panic, feeling a Plexiglas wall
between them.

(*Suddenly, screaming.*) Mom! Mom! *Mom!*

The energy is enough to propel Sophie from her world
and into the 'real' world. We are now in real time, real
place: Sophie's bedroom, sitting on the edge of her
bed, shivering, sweating. Calliope comes in. It's the
middle of the night.

Calliope (*bleary*) Sophie!

Sophie I had the Fear.

Calliope It's OK.

She gets on the bed and hugs Sophie. She's done this
before.

Here you are. You're real. It's OK.

Sophie (*grateful*) How's it fucking OK? OK is the exact
opposite of what it is.

Calliope (*stroking Sophie's hair*) Do you want me to get
Judy?

Sophie (*scornful*) Judy.

Calliope Or get you a tablet?

Sophie No. They make me so thick and blurry. Just . . .
stay for a bit.

Calliope OK.

Sophie And don't stop. I think I understand why cats
purr. Wouldn't it be nice to be a cat? You could be as
independent as you liked, go out chasing mice or
whatever, and then when you wanted you could just
climb on to someone's lap and let them stroke you.
Maybe I'll come back as a cat.

Calliope stops abruptly.

Calliope Don't, Soph.

Sophie What?

Calliope 'Reincarnation'. You sound like Judy.

Sophie So?

Calliope So, first of all there's no such thing –

Sophie (*interrupting*) Fuck off. You don't know any better than she does.

Calliope Um, I so do.

Sophie You do not.

Calliope Sophie –

Sophie (*mocking*) 'Calliope' –

Calliope (*raising her voice*) And second of all it's not helpful to think like that.

Sophie (*getting angry*) Well maybe I'll come back as a bat and tangle myself in your hair. Or a mosquito. Or maybe I'll just come back as a ghost and haunt you till your dying day. No matter how fast you run or how far you go you'll never be able to get away from me.

Calliope Stop it, Sophie.

Sophie 'Stop it, Sophie!'

Calliope I'm being serious.

Sophie 'I'm being serious!'

Calliope Shut up!

Sophie Shut up? Fuck off! Fuck off, Peace Warrior. I'm the one who's fucking dying here.

Calliope If you could only hear yourself –

Daphne enters.

Daphne Girls.

Calliope Sophie couldn't sleep.

Sophie I couldn't sleep.

Daphne Well, I don't think that's any excuse for you to be gallivanting around in here, Calliope. (*Tuts her disapproval.*) Keeping your sister awake. She needs her rest, and you – you've got school tomorrow.

Sophie starts to giggle. Calliope catches her eye and starts to giggle too. Daphne is flustered and awkward.

Well now. Well now, really. I fail to see how any of what I've just said is funny.

Sophie and Calliope are snorting now, trying to stifle their laughter. Daphne is miserable and awkward.

Calliope Calliope. I'm asking you, nicely –

Sophie (*an impression of Daphne*) 'To stop gallivanting about and go to bed.'

Daphne Sophie!

Sophie (*an impression of Daphne*) 'To be fresh-faced and bushy-tailed for school.'

Daphne Well, really, I –
I would have expected better of you, Calliope.

Daphne turns abruptly and goes.
Sophie howls with laughter. Calliope isn't laughing any more.

Calliope That was mean of us. She tries, Daphne.

Sophie Whose side are you on?

Calliope Nobody's. It's not about 'sides'. (*She sighs.*) Of course I'm on yours, Soph. But Daphne's right. You had better get some rest.

Sophie I've got the entire whole of eternity to rest.

Calliope You'll be wrecked tomorrow.

Sophie Give a shit?

She wriggles away from Calliope.

Who died and made you Daphne?

Calliope giggles. Sophie giggles, reluctantly.

Calliope Come on. Shall I tuck you in?

Sophie Remember that place in Goa? Where the kids all slept in one room, and the grown-ups in another? How old were we then?

Calliope (*shrugs*) Seven? Well, I was seven. So you were four.

Sophie You used to tuck me in and give me pretend hot milk, like we'd seen the mum do on some film. And then –

Calliope Sophie.

Sophie What? It's just us.

Calliope I don't care. What did I tell you? You don't repeat any of it to anyone, ever.

Sophie If I really couldn't sleep –

Calliope Sophie –

Sophie You used to let me pretend I was a baby and suck your titty. It's a nice memory, I want to remember! We were children, Cal. I'm sure loads of children do stuff like that. You'll see. You'll have children one day and –

Calliope Never having children. Being serious.

Sophie You will. (*Wistful.*) You'll have sex and boyfriends and babies and – everything, all of it.

Calliope They think I'm a weirdo, Sophie. They all do. They found out my real name and they all call me Flower Power. (*She stops abruptly.*) Sorry. It's none of your business.

Sophie How is it none of my business? You're my sister. I'll come back as a ghost and haunt *them*.

Calliope We really should go to sleep, Soph.

Sophie OK, Daphne. OK, *Mother*. Go on, goodnight.

Calliope Night.

Calliope leaves. Sophie sits up and looks after her.

TWO

Sophie in her 'space' again. The others in their spaces, as before.

Sophie Friday the 18th of September. It's been more than a week. It's been eleven days, in fact. I haven't been well. I took a fever in the night, and they had to take me to hospital. I had isolation, IVs, the works, and then another blood transfusion, even though the last one was only two weeks ago. They said they'll last less and less now, the transfusions. They wanted to keep me in longer. But I just wanted to be home.

'Home'. This isn't my home. I don't know where I'd say my home is, if I had to say. Funny, though. Judy always called here 'home', no matter how far we were from it, no matter me and Cal had never even seen it. Wherever we were existed only in relation to here, which is a funny thought, when you get here, and see all it is, how ordinary, forgettable.

But I'm glad to be back here.

I'm not going to show you hospital. I'm not going to show you any of the bad stuff, if I can help it. I don't want the bad stuff to be remembered.

Sometimes, if I'm honest, it feels like there's nothing else. Dying is a long, slow, messy, boring, complicated, repetitive business. The oxygen tank and the tablets, the stacks of gauze and sanitiser . . . The sponge baths and sick-basin . . . The bowls of chicken soup and hot milk, the mashed potato, a spoon at a time . . . There's a nurse who comes every other day, sent by Macmillan. She – it's usually a she, though once it was a he – cleans my port (*IV port on her chest*) and takes blood samples and asks if I want to talk about how I'm feeling. I thought of showing you that. But I don't think I'm going to. I don't want the crap stuff and the smelly stuff and the painful stuff to live on. I don't want you to see me farting and bleeding and rotting from the inside out. The good thing is that smell doesn't travel – there's no way of preserving smell – and smell's the worst thing of all. No matter how much of Daphne's granny-perfume I spray or Judy's sandalwood I burn you can still smell it, sometimes like a whiff of bad eggs and sometimes faint and stale, like flakes of dry skin on clothes that have lain heaped in a cupboard too long.

It's very lonely, dying. Knowing how bad you smell, and watching people determined not to notice it. You want to say to them, to shout at them, I can smell it too and it's fucking disgusting! I'm as grossed-out as you are, more, because it's coming from me!

I'm not going to talk about that any more. I'm not going to talk about that any more.

A moment. She regains control.

You're not going to see me, either, as I really am at the moment. Because that's not me – that's the illness. I'm so spindly and pale a puff of wind could blow me away, and since I decided I didn't want any more treatment my hair has grown back fluffy and soft, like the fuzz on a newborn chick, or a dandelion. I don't look at myself in mirrors any more, and I don't like it when I see my reflection in the dark glass of a window. Because it's not me. It's some girl, some very ill girl who looks about nine or ten, with eyes like saucers and ribs like a xylophone. You're seeing me as I see me, as I want to see me, not how any of the others see me. That's a comfort to me. Because the way they see me, what I know they're seeing when they look at me, it does my head in.

So. As Daphne would say, thank heaven for small mercies.

Stupid Daphne.

She turns to Daphne, who is praying.

She's redoubled her efforts since I was last hospitalised. She comes in at night and whispers prayers, when she thinks I'm asleep. I hate it. I fucking hate it.

Calliope stands suddenly. Turns, and marches in to Daphne.

Calliope I want you to stop praying for her.

Daphne Beg pardon?

Calliope You heard. I said, I want you to stop praying for her.

Daphne Calliope –

Calliope Because it's no use! It's no fucking use, Daphne! I've been reading your Bible, you know. (*Snatches up Daphne's Bible.*) I've been reading it. Here, listen to this.

She riffles through and finds the gospel of John.

John, chapter fourteen. 'I will do whatever you ask in my name, so that the Son may bring glory to the Father.' This is Jesus, Daphne. This is Jesus's words! 'You may ask me for anything in my name, and I will do it.' OK then. God! Jesus! Are you listening? Because I'm going to ask you something. I'm going to ask for my sister Sophie to get better. Because she's only thirteen, God. It's so unfair. She's my only sister and she's more than a sister, she's my best friend. She's my only friend. We've always done everything together, always. And I've always looked after her. I've always protected her, and made sure no one hurts her. I've taught her how to read and I've tucked her in at night. So now I'm asking you – in your own words – in your own name – to not let her die. OK, God? Do you hear me?

Calliope is weeping. Daphne holds her, hugs her.

Daphne It's all right, it's all right.

Calliope It's not all right, Daphne! It's not fucking all right. She's my sister. What are we going to do, Daphne? What are we going to do?

Calliope collapses again.
Daphne holds her.
Sophie watches.

Sophie Nobody talks about afterwards. Not in front of me, anyway. But it's what they're all thinking, even as they hate themselves for thinking about it. Calliope's going to stay here, I reckon. All she's ever wanted is to be normal. In all the places we were, however we were living, whatever we were doing, all she wanted was to be unexceptional. She's going to stay here with Daphne, and carry on at school, and the rest of it. She'll probably have my bedroom. They'll clean it out and do it up new and it'll become Calliope's. I don't know what will happen to Judy. I don't think Judy knows what will happen to Judy. She can't stay here, it's too small for her. But she can't run away for ever.

Sophie turns to watch Judy. Judy is standing, alone.
   The scene between Daphne and Calliope has dissolved now. The clock strikes five. They set about 'preparing' tea time, exactly as before. Judy walks in; they all sit down. Sophie follows her in.

Daphne Dear Lord – (*Long pause.*)

They eat. Sophie watches. The only dialogue is the following.

Daphne Pass the salt please, Calliope.

Calliope Pass the butter, Judy?

Judy The pepper?

THREE

Sophie, Judy and Daphne are all back in their spaces. But this time, Calliope is in Daphne's space.

Sophie Wednesday, 23rd of September.
   There was a game we used to play when we were little, on the ashram in Kerala. There were about twenty kids, and while our parents meditated and practised the Death of the Self we played dying, too. I was always best. We played it in the airing cupboard of the laundry room. The grown-ups banned it, but we played it anyway. The way it worked was: you had to get down on your back, hands crossed over your chest, like a corpse, and wriggle backwards in. You had to stay in as long as possible, and the one who managed longest was the winner. There was no room to move in there. If you lifted your head even a tiny bit your nose scraped the underside of the rough wooden planks. Your mind played tricks, like you thought you saw shadows clawing at your face or black spiders creeping up from the holes in the floor. Bit by bit

it got harder to breathe, and it felt as if the top and sides were pressing in on you, like soil being shovelled into a grave, and someone was stamping it down, tighter and tighter, and even if you only took little sips of air it was earth and your lungs were full of dust and suddenly you'd panic. And it was then you'd get hurt. The only way out was to kick the door with your foot and the others would be listening for it and they'd open up and drag you out by the ankles. If you forgot and tried to sit up or scramble out by yourself you'd hit your head and get splinters in your hands and all sorts.

No one ever beat me because I worked out the secret. The secret was, you had to think yourself elsewhere. It was easy, once you knew how. You had to concentrate on breathing in as slowly as you could, and with every breath out you had to feel yourself leaving your body, you had to push yourself out a little more each time and think yourself somewhere else. I used to choose the swings in a playground we'd once played in. I got so good at it that I could really and truly feel the wind in my hair as I swung, backwards and forwards, higher and higher, rushing and swooping and falling through the air.

Sophie looks at Calliope's space. It is very dimly lit: Calliope is no longer there.

I tried to explain to Calliope how it worked, but she never understood me.

The clock strikes five. The same routine. But no grace this time.

Daphne Pass the salt please, Calliope.

Calliope Pass the butter, Judy?

Judy The pepper?

Then suddenly Calliope breaks the routine.

36

Calliope Daphne –

The others turn to her, surprised.

Can I go out tonight?

Daphne Out?

Calliope Only to the cinema. With –
With some people from school.

Daphne Well, I –
I don't see why not.

Judy You've made friends, Peace?

Calliope (*flushed and awkward*) Not Peace, Judy. How
many times –

Judy Sorry. 'Cal'. You've made friends, 'Cal'?

Calliope Yeah, sort of. Not really. I mean –

Sophie It's a boy? You're such a bad liar, Calliope.
You're meeting a boy.

*Daphne rummages for her purse, takes a note and
pushes it into Calliope's reluctant hand.*

Daphne You go and enjoy yourself, love. Put everything
else out of your mind. God knows you deserve a little
fun.

Calliope But . . . what about Sophie?

Daphne Sophie won't mind.

Calliope But –

Daphne She'll be fine. She won't even realise you're
gone.

Calliope You really think it's OK?

Daphne Go, Calliope.

Judy Go, Calliope.

Calliope That's the first time I've heard you two united. (*She stands.*) I'm going to take my phone with me. I'm going to keep it on loud. You're to ring me, OK? The second that –

Daphne She'll be fine. We'll all be fine. Go on with you.

Calliope OK.

Calliope leaves the kitchen. But then she turns suddenly and goes into Sophie's bedroom. Sophie follows her in. Sophie is 'there' by the time the following exchange happens.

Sophie It's a boy, isn't it?

Calliope How did you know?

Sophie What's his name?

Calliope Nadeem. He sits next to me in French and Spanish. I've been helping him.

Sophie You've taken such a reddener.

Calliope I have not!

Sophie You have so, I can feel the heat from here! Ow, get away from me, Cal, you're burning me! (*She stops playing.*) Are you going to do it with him?

Calliope Philosophy! I hardly know him! And it's not a date-date, anyway, it's just the cinema.

Sophie What are you going to see?

Calliope I don't know. We're just meeting there at half past seven and we'll see. (*Pause.*) Is it OK, Soph?

Sophie What do you mean?

Calliope You know what I mean. Is it OK, if I go?

Sophie Course it is. I'm not your Daphne.

Calliope I'll tell you all about it.

Sophie Go on. Go.

Calliope leaves. Sophie watches her go.
Sophie is small.
Judy and Daphne are still in the kitchen.
Sophie wanders in to them.

Daphne You're not even thirty-five, Judy. Heaven's sakes. You're not even thirty-bloody-five, pardon my French. There's still time. You can meet a nice man, settle down.

Judy (*standing*) Mom –

Daphne I've never understood what the matter with you is, Judy.

Judy No, Mom. You've never understood me. You or Dad. You never did. All you cared about was church on Sunday, and manners, and what the neighbours thought. You only liked me when I fitted in with how you thought I should be. How you wanted people to see you. 'Meet a nice man, settle down.'

Daphne But you could, Judy. Instead of, instead of putting yourself through this exile from yourself. It's never too late to change your mind about things. About what you want, or what's important.

Judy What's important is that my child is dying.

Daphne I lost a child too, Judy. Not in the same way, but I lost a child too, my only child.

Judy What? You mean –
How – how dare you, Mom? How dare you?

Daphne When your father took the stroke I had no way of getting word to you. No way of knowing where in the world you were. And my own grandchildren. Knowing I had grandchildren in the world and –

Judy I can't do this now, Daphne. I just can't do this now.

Judy turns and marches out, back to her space. Daphne sits back down, head in hands. Sophie wanders over to Judy.

Sophie You could, you know. She's right.

Judy 'Meet a nice man, settle down.'

Sophie You could.

Judy 'Not even thirty-five yet.' (*Beat.*) I'm not.

Sophie Have a whole new family. Have a baby. Start again. You could, couldn't you? The thought is actually crossing your mind.

Sophie panics.

Judy. Judy!

Judy cannot hear her.

FOUR

They are all in Sophie's room. Sophie is in her space, watching them.

Sophie Monday 28th of September, Saturday 3rd of October. Saturday 10th of October, Wednesday 14th of October. Another transfusion, another. They're lasting less than a week now. Sunday 18th of October, Thursday 22nd. Monday 26th and Thursday 29th. The first of November.

I'm still not speaking to Judy. Whenever she comes into my room, I turn to face the wall, or pretend to be asleep. (*Mimicking.*) Do you want a massage, Philosophy? Shall

I light some of this nice incense? Shall I help you with your visualisations? (*As herself.*) Fuck off, Judy, fuck off, Judy, fuck off, Judy.

I hate her. I hate everyone. I hate the world.

(*Suddenly, vehemently.*) Get away from me, all of you. Get away from here.

> *She jumps at them, waving her arms, and chases them out of her bedroom. Calliope back to the attic, Judy to the shed, Daphne to the kitchen.*
>
> *A clock strikes five. Nobody moves but Sophie.*

(*Mockingly.*) Pass the salt please, Calliope. Pass the butter, Judy? The pepper?

> *The clock strikes five again. Calliope stands. She walks into Sophie's bedroom. This is 'real'.*

Calliope What are you doing, Sophie?

Sophie (*sullen*) What?

Calliope You can't keep this up.

Sophie Watch me.

> *Sophie turns to the wall, her back to Calliope. Calliope sits down on the bed.*

Calliope Come on, Soph.

Sophie Don't touch me.

Calliope Come on. (*Pause.*) She's at her wits' end, Sophie. She doesn't know what you're punishing her for.

Sophie Then she's stupid. You all are. Thick as pigshit, the lot of you.

Calliope She cries herself to sleep every night, Soph. Every single night. I have to lie there listening to her. She buries her head in her sleeping bag and thinks I don't hear her.

41

Sophie Good.

Calliope Sophie . . . This isn't you. This isn't my sister.
I'm the one who fights with Judy, for God's sake. You're
the one who sticks up for her, who – who listens to her
crazy theories about crystals and Freeganism. What has
she done?

> *Sophie is silent.*

I'm being serious, Sophie. What has she done? And
whatever it is – can you not just – be kind to her? Or a
little bit kinder?

Sophie That's rich, Peace Warrior, coming from you.
Think of all the fights you've had with her. Think of how
many times you've kept me up all night telling me how
mad you are with her. Think of that time in the warehouse
in London you hatched a plan to give the two of us up to
Social Services. You're such a hypocrite.

> *Calliope says nothing.*

Have you finished now? Because if you have, please do
me a favour and fuck off.

Calliope Sophie –

> *But then Calliope breaks off, turns and leaves the
> room without another word.*

Sophie She was, you know. Going to go to Social Services.
The only thing that stopped her was the thought that we
mightn't be kept together.

> *Sophie stops, abruptly. She turns her back.*
>   *But the action continues. Calliope has not gone back
> into her space. She is standing, thinking. She makes a
> decision. Calliope walks into Judy's shed. She stops.*

Judy Is everything OK?

Calliope Yeah. (*Beat.*) God, Judy.

Judy What?

Calliope (*flapping her hand in front of her face*) Stinks in here. I can hardly see my own hand. No wonder you're permanently wasted. Thirty seconds in here I'm going to be frosted. Dope fiend. (*Beat.*) You were meant to be giving up.

Judy I am. I have. I'm out, Peace. Cashed.

She hands Calliope her tin, open. It is empty. Calliope takes it, shakes it.

Promise.

Calliope Since when did you give up?

Judy Yesterday.

Calliope rolls her eyes.

I tipped it down the drain, all of it. (*Beat.*) It was lemonade, anyway, that stuff. Lipton tea.

Calliope So what are you still out here for, if you're not getting high?

Judy (*attempt at joke*) Being low?

Calliope doesn't laugh.

Calliope You could come inside. Why d'you not, anyway? It's cold out here, and it stinks. You should come inside.

Judy Pee-wee –

Calliope How many times do I have to tell you –

Judy Sorry. I keep forgetting. 'Cal'. 'Callie' and 'Sophie'. (*Beat.*) Sit on the sofa, Sophie. (*Beat.*) I went to the Job Centre this morning.

Sophie turns around at this point. Stares at them.

Calliope You what?

Judy Yep. Went down the Job Centre. Institute Road. Used to pass it every day, never thought I'd end up there. It was a lad from school running it. Billy Hagan. He knew me as soon as I gave my name. (*Impression of him.*) 'Judy Cunningham? Bloody hell, ladies and gents, if it isn't Judy bloody Cunningham! And to what do we owe the honour? I thought you were on the hippy trail. Like one of them Hairy Krishnas.' On and on he went, in front of everyone. And then he said, 'What brings you back here?' and I said, 'I'm looking for a job.' And he said, 'No, seriously, *Kings Heath*.' And I didn't know what to say, Calliope.

Calliope Yeah.

Sophie (*bitterly*) I have been more places and seen more things than the limitations of your world will even allow for.

Calliope So what did you do?

Judy I said, 'My daughter's been diagnosed with Stage 3 Osteosarcoma, which is a rare type of bone cancer, and they've been treating her at the Heartlands.' (*She laughs, mirthlessly.*) That shut him up.

Calliope And then what?

Judy He was so embarrassed he couldn't even look me in the eye.

Calliope Tell me about it.

Sophie scowls at them.

Sophie (*at Calliope*) Traitor.

Judy He couldn't get out of there fast enough. Called over someone else to register me, and the rest of it. (*Beat.*) They offered me a job as a shelf-stacker slash merchandiser.

Calliope A shelf-stacker slash merchandiser?

Sophie bursts out laughing, cruelly.
Calliope laughs, despite herself.
Judy laughs.
Sophie stops when Judy laughs.

Judy 'Duties include filling of shelves of company products and working to certain retail procedures.' Eight hours a day, temporary leading to permanent, minimum wage.

Calliope Jeez, Judy.

Judy I told them I could cook. You have to go through a questionnaire, where you list your life experience and skills. And I said I've regularly cooked for twenty, fifty, one hundred people. And the woman said, 'But have you got your Basic Food Hygiene Certificate?' And then she took pity on me and she said, there must be something else you can do, and I told her I could get by in three or four languages, grow food, and make things, and mend things – remember the bags we used to sew, out of cloth scraps? And the jewellery?

Calliope says nothing. She is deeply embarrassed for Judy.

A shelf-stacker slash merchandiser. (*Beat.*) Alternatively I can take a Skills Course, in the daytime. Learn typing, and spreadsheets, and basic computer use. And if I can locate and bring in my GCSE certificates, they can fast-track me on to an Office Administration Programme.

Calliope Well then, there you go!

Judy looks at her.

Sophie Can you really see Judy doing an Office Administration course, Peace Warrior? Setting off every day in her cheap suit from the supermarket, or the

Salvation Army, to learn typing and spreadsheets and basic office management? (*She laughs.*) You could cut her hair, do her make-up for her. Teach her how to walk in high heels instead of Birkenstocks. You'd like that. You've always wanted to normalise her.

Calliope What else are you going to do, Judy?

Judy I don't know. I don't know. (*Beat.*) You're happy here, aren't you?

Calliope 'Happy'?

Judy Aside from that. Apart from – all of that. You want to stay here, don't you?

Calliope Yeah. I do.

Judy sighs, closes her eyes.
Silence.

(*Shyly.*) Judy.

Judy opens her eyes.

I found your diary. In a shoebox, in the attic. (*She produces it.*) From when you were sixteen going on seventeen. My age.

Judy takes it, slowly, turns it over in her hands.

Judy Have you been reading it?

Calliope No. (*Beat.*) Bits of it. Not all, not properly.

Sophie Liar.

Judy opens it, flicks through it.

Judy 'Saturday the 4th September, 1993. I've bought a pregnancy test from Boots the Chemist and I'm going to do it tomorrow morning. It says it's more accurate if you do it in the morning. Which means there's the whole night to wait. I was meant to be going out with Lou and

Emma but I told them I thought I was coming down with something. I said that to Mom and Dad too and now I'm sitting up in my bedroom listening to them watching *Blind Date* downstairs with nowhere to go and no one to turn to. I can see some kids playing on the swings with their moms and the moms are getting ready to go because it's getting dark and it's their bedtime or whatever and the kids don't want to go and watching it is making me feel sick and sad all at the same time.'

Judy stops. Riffles on through the pages.

'December 21st. I want this baby and nothing anyone says is going to change my mind. Dad says I'm not his daughter any more. Mom says how can she hold her head up in front of anyone ever again. I don't care. I'll run away. I'll –'

Judy stops abruptly. Closes the diary.

I don't think I want to read any more.

Calliope It's weird, isn't it? You're my age. (*Beat.*) You're really convinced you wanted me, aren't you? All the way through. Despite – everything.

Sophie I thought you said you hadn't read it.

Judy I wanted to give you exactly the life I didn't have.

She looks around her and starts to laugh. Calliope starts to laugh.

(*Suddenly.*) My dad used to come out here and smoke cigarettes and my mom pretended she didn't notice. He was meant to have given up. He allowed himself one a week, on a Saturday evening. I knew where he kept his pack and I used to steal them and he couldn't say anything, because he wasn't meant to be smoking, either.

Calliope Can I keep this?

47

Judy Can you keep it? Have you not got enough teenage angst of your own?

Calliope It's just funny, thinking of you as me. I've never thought of you like that before. (*Beat.*) And I'd have it. For when you go off wherever you're going to go.

Judy says nothing. Then slowly hands Calliope the diary. Calliope takes it.

Thank you. (*Suddenly.*) I think you should go back to Findhorn, Judy. Where we spent that summer, on the west of Scotland. There was a community there, and they were good people. Not like those weirdos you fell in with in London and Cornwall. Your problem is you're too trusting of people. But Findhorn – it had integrity. It was genuine. I think you'd be happy there. And – and it wouldn't be too far, either. (*She breaks off.*)

A moment. Judy looks at her, puzzled, wonderingly.

Judy Thank you, Calliope.

Calliope (*shrugs, awkward*) It's OK.

Sophie is watching intently. Judy and Calliope slow down, fade out, slightly.

Sophie You're moving on. You're making up and making friends, confiding in each other. Making plans for afterwards. Out loud, in broad daylight! How can you? How dare you? What about me?

She is screaming but they don't hear her. She tries to get to them, but she cannot reach.

I hate you, Judy! And I hate you, Calliope! I hate you both! I hate you all!

She runs at them, flapping her arms, as she did before, but it has no impact on them this time.

(*In a cold rage.*) The second of November, the third. The fourth, the sixth, the seventh. The tenth and seventeenth. Transfusion, transfusion. My bones and blood are riddled with it now. I wish it was infectious. I'd give it to Judy. I'd give it to all of them. I'm not talking to any of them, now.

One by one, they all come into Sophie's bedroom and stand there, keeping vigil. She is not there. Silence.
Then suddenly, Daphne talks. The others cannot hear her.

Daphne I've had enough of you, madam. I really have. I know it's hard. I know hard's not even the right word, that it doesn't even come close. I know I can't even begin to imagine what you're going through, what it's like being you. But what do you think it's like being us? What do you think it's like being your mother, your poor mother, trying her best, and you giving her nothing but hatred and the silent treatment? What do you think it's like being Calliope, or me? Why are you doing this, Sophie? Why are you doing it?

Sophie (*shouting back from her space*) You want to know? You want to know why? It's so you won't miss me, Daphne. It's so none of you will miss me, when I'm gone.
I'll be gone. And you still here. Get away from me, Daphne. Get away from me, all of you.

Daphne You can't keep on doing this. We're part of you, Sophie. Your mother and your sister – and yes, me, even me. We're all part of it. It's us, too, don't you understand? Please, Sophie? Please?

Sophie is standing, pale and small in her space.

Sophie The twenty-first of November, the twenty-second, third. My time is running out. Sand in an hourglass, or water in your cupped hands. I wake up one morning while it's still dark, and watch the light seep in, and realise I can't do this any more. Daphne's right. And the hatred has disappeared, like night-mist as the sun rises, a ground-frost melting. I don't know why, or how. I just know I can't do this any more.

FIVE

Sophie enters the kitchen. It is the 'real' her, now, and 'real' time.

Sophie Daphne?

Daphne Sophie, heavens! What are you doing up? Poor little love, let's get you back to bed.

Sophie No, Daphne, please, this is important. I can't do it any more. I want to say I'm sorry.

Daphne Sorry? Oh, love. Oh, my love. You have nothing to be sorry for, nothing.

Sophie But I do, Daphne, I do. So I want to say sorry, and the other thing –
   There's another thing, that I want you to promise me. And it's very important, really very important. So I need you to promise.

Daphne I'll do my best.

Sophie No, I need a promise.

Daphne I think you'd better tell me what this is.

Sophie It's – it's –
   Will you promise not to close the curtains? Not fully, anyway. And will you promise always to leave a crack of the window open?

Daphne It's the middle of winter, Sophie. I can't leave the windows open. The gas bill will be horrendous. We may as well –

Sophie (*interrupting*) Please. I can't explain. It's just important, you have no idea how important it is. Please will you promise me, and will you make sure the others do it, too? I know I can trust you. I'm asking you because I know I can trust you.

A moment.

Daphne All right, then. I promise.

Sophie OK. Until Christmas is over, right? No closed curtains, no closed windows.

Daphne No closed curtains, no closed windows. I promise.

Sophie Thank you.

Daphne Come here, little 'un.

She hugs Sophie.
   Then Sophie moves away, out of the space.
   Daphne sits back down at the kitchen table. Sophie watches her for a moment.

Sophie I wish I could have known you, Daphne. I wish you could have been my nan.

Then she turns and watches Judy. After a while:

I'm sorry, Mom. You've been a pretty fucking shoddy mom, at times. But I'm sorry I haven't been a better daughter.

Judy sighs, straightens up.

Judy If you lose your parents you're orphaned. If you lose your spouse you're widowed. But there is no word for what it means to lose your child. It's as if – as if it's too terrible even for language to allow.

Sophie goes to her, palms out, as if she can almost touch her. But the glass wall is in the way. A moment. Then Judy leaves 'her' space and goes into Sophie's bedroom. Sophie watches her go, then follows her, gets there just before her mother. When Judy enters, it is as if Sophie has just woken up.

Sophie (*bleary*) Judy?

Judy Shh, bab. I haven't woken you, have I? I didn't mean to. You just go back to sleep.

She sets about drawing the curtains. A clock is striking five.

Sophie Not the curtains, Mom. Not the windows and curtains.

Judy (*stops, collects herself*) I'm sorry. I forgot. I won't again.

She opens the curtains part way. Then she sits down by Sophie, strokes her forehead.

Sophie Will you read to me?

Judy Will I read to you?

Sophie I always used to want that, when we were little. For you just to read a book to us.

Judy I did read to you. Well, I didn't *read*-read, but I told you stories.

Sophie I know. They were brilliant stories. But sometimes I just wanted you to say the words that were on the page.

Judy nods, slowly.

I found some books. Well, Calliope found them, in the attic. Old ones of yours. There's *Watership Down*, *Charlotte's Web*. And *Little Women* . . . The teacher read us that in school, in San Francisco. Calliope loved it. I've been reading it now, only I've got so tired, Mom, my eyes are swimmy. Will you read it for me?

Judy (*dubiously, flicking through it*) *Little Women*?

Sophie We all know what you think of *Little Women*, Judy.

Judy I mean –

Sophie It's soppy, sentimental, manipulative, etcetera, etcetera. Please?

Judy (*beat*) Of course.

Sophie hands her the book – a battered hardback. She flicks through it, then opens it and begins to read.

' "Christmas won't be Christmas without any presents," grumbled Jo, lying on the –'

Sophie (*interrupts*) No, not from there. The second part. Page three-nine-five.

Judy Page three-nine-five?

She looks at Sophie, then flicks forward, finds the page. Reads it, silently. Looks at Sophie. Beat.

Philosophy –

Sophie Please?

Judy I'm sorry. I'm not reading this. I can't.

Sophie But please?

Judy is unable to read. Sophie closes her eyes and recites.

' "I love you more than anyone else in the world, Beth," said Jo. "I used to think I couldn't let you go, but I'm learning to feel that I don't lose you, that you'll be more to me than ever, and death can't part us, though it seems to." '

Daphne is laying the table for dinner. But in 'her' space, Calliope is standing, looking towards the bedroom. She walks towards them, slowly, enters the room.

' "I know it cannot," said Beth, "and I don't fear it any longer, for I'm sure I shall be your Beth still, to love and help you more than ever." '

Calliope *(softly) Little Women*. The teacher in San Francisco –

Sophie You remember?

Calliope Of course I remember. You stole the book for me when we moved on. You got in so much trouble for that.

Calliope gets onto the bed, beside Sophie and Judy. She takes the book from Judy and finds the chapter.

' "You must take my place, Jo, and be everything to Father and Mother when I'm gone. They will turn to you, don't fail them, and if it's hard to work alone, remember that I don't forget you, and that you'll be happier in doing that than writing splendid books or seeing all the world, for love is the only thing that we can carry with us when we go, and it makes the going easy." So the spring days –' (*She falters, clears her throat.*) 'So the spring days – the spring days –' (*She breaks off.*)

Judy takes the book.

Judy 'The spring days came and went, the sky grew clearer, the earth greener, the flowers were up fairly early, and the birds came back in time to say goodbye to Beth, who, like a tired but trustful child, clung to the hands that had led her all her life, as –' (*Beat. Distasteful.*)

'Father and Mother guided her tenderly through the Valley of the Shadow, and – gave her up to God.'

Daphne is there. Like Calliope, she has stood, facing the bedroom from 'her' space, then has made her way towards it.

Daphne *Little Women.* I loved those books.

Calliope So did me and Soph! Judy hated them.

Daphne Don't stop on my account. I didn't mean to interrupt. (*Beat.*) You're reading from *Good Wives*, aren't you? The part where –

Judy Sophie asked for it. (*Determined to finish.*) 'Seldom except in books do the dying utter memorable words, see visions, or depart with beatified countenances, and those who have sped many parting souls know that to most the end comes as naturally and simply as sleep. As Beth had hoped, the "tide went out easily", and in the dark hour before dawn, on the bosom where she had drawn her first breath, she quietly drew her last, with no farewell but one loving look, one little sigh.'

Sophie You're almost there. Don't stop.

Judy 'When morning came, for the first time in many months the fire was out, Jo's place was empty, and the room was very still. But a bird sang blithely on a budding bough, close by, the snowdrops blossomed freshly at the window, and the spring sunshine streamed in like a benediction over the placid face upon the pillow, a face so full of painless peace that those who loved it best smiled through their tears, and –'

Calliope 'Thanked God that Beth was well at last.'

Daphne *Little* bloody *Women.* Remember I read that to you, Judy, and you'd have none of it? Raged at me, so she did, girls: why should the little women have to keep house all day and look after the menfolk? And what's this you've got here? (*She is bustling.*) *Watership Down? Charlotte's Web?*

Sophie Calliope found them in the attic.

Daphne That bleeding *Charlotte's Web*'s what made your mom a vegetarian. Oh, the rows we had! Do you remember, Judy? The rows we had! And your poor father, God rest him. Slamming his hands on the table. (*She starts to laugh. Roars, does an impression of him.*) 'Vegetarian? I've never heard such bloody nonsense in me life. You hate vegetables.'

She is laughing. Judy is laughing. Calliope smiles. Sophie smiles, weakly.

Well, girls. Tea's ready. I'll bring you yours up, Sophie.

Calliope (*suddenly*) Can we all have it here?

Daphne Have our tea? Up here?

Calliope Can we, though?

Daphne Well, I –

Sophie Please.

Daphne Well. Only if it doesn't tire Sophie out. All right, Sophie? The second you start to feel tired, or want us out of here –

Sophie I won't do.

Daphne You will, and you're to tell us. OK? (*To the rest of them.*) And you're not to go getting crumbs everywhere, and mess. I changed the sheets only this morning. Oh, this is the most ridiculous idea I've ever heard. We're not flippin' campers, are we . . . ?

She carries on grumbling as she leaves.

Judy (*suddenly*) Thank you, Mom.

Daphne (*surprised*) You what, love?

Judy Thank you. For – for –

They look at each other for a moment. Daphne nods, slowly.

Daphne Thank you.

Daphne turns rapidly and bustles out. The scene fades. Judy follows Daphne into the kitchen. Calliope leaves the stage entirely. Sophie gets up and goes to 'her' space.

Sophie I can feel it, twisting and twisting in my bones. There isn't much of me left. I'm glad you got to see that.

She turns and watches the others. Daphne and Judy are sitting together in the kitchen. She watches them for a while. The lights dim on them; they stop moving. She turns to Calliope's space. Calliope is gone. She watches Calliope's space for a while. A clock strikes midnight. Calliope appears, excited, furtive. She makes her way to Sophie's bedroom, tiptoeing so that no one can see her, making sure nobody hears her. She kneels by the bed. Sophie watches from her space.

Calliope Oh, Sophie, I know you're asleep, but I just had to tell you! (*She is breathless and excited, giggles.*) I mean you asked me to tell you, and I promised I would. Right. Well . . . (*She giggles again.*) I did it, Sophie! I did it with Nadeem! And it was . . . amaaaaazing.

Sophie is watching, small and still.

His mother and father went to the mosque, and his brother and sister were out somewhere, so we went up to his room . . . and we just did it, we 'made love'! We were dead careful, though, don't worry about that! It's crazy to think that Judy was only my age, when she had me. We used a condom *and* he pulled out before he came, just to be extra safe. And afterwards we just lay there, and I didn't say I loved him, because it might have been too much, but I felt it. And he was the same, I know he was. And he just kept stroking my stomach, Soph, and kissing my neck with the softest little kisses. We're going to go to Greece in the summer, he says, but not to look for my dad or anything like that. Just to go, for a holiday, Crete, maybe. We looked at places on the internet. Oh, I wish you could meet him, Soph!

Sophie Did it hurt?

Calliope (*almost overlapping*) It didn't hurt, not one bit. Everyone says it does, but it didn't. He was dead gentle, though, maybe that was why. I had this moment, though, Soph, of looking at his cock and going, 'Oh My God. That's never going to fit inside me!' (*She dissolves into fits of giggles.*)

Sophie But what was it *like*, Cal? What was it . . . *like*?

Calliope Oh, it was – it was – amaaaazing!

Sophie You're going to grow up, now. You're growing up already, away from me. Soon you're going to look back and realise that you've lived my life twice over. It'll seem to happen in a flash and you'll think: how did that happen? You'll be married by then, maybe to Nadeem, maybe someone else, and next thing you'll have babies, and they won't be babies any longer, and you'll be reading stories to them in bed. And they'll be my age and you'll tell them about me but not too much because you won't want to frighten them. You'll just say: I had a sister, but she died young.

This is the closest we ever see Sophie to tears.

I hate you, Calliope. I fucking hate you. Make sure you make the most of it. Make sure you don't waste a moment of it. I sound like bloody Daphne.

Calliope, standing up, more sober.

Calliope Well, I promised I'd tell you. I hope this counts.
Goodnight, Sophie. I love you.

Calliope leaves her bedroom.

SIX

Daphne, Judy, Calliope in Sophie's bedroom.

Sophie Thursday 3rd December.
  This is what will happen next.
  I'll get weaker and weaker and tireder and tireder until
I slip away, and it'll be just like falling asleep. This will
take a few days, maybe as much as two weeks, depending.
I'm not going to make it to Christmas.
  I won't be hungry any more, and I won't be thirsty,
either. I'll be able to hear right up until the end, and it
won't be painful because of the morphine.
  That's what the nurse says.
  I don't believe her.
  Being born is painful – just think of babies, they come
out all covered in blood and slime, screaming at the
shock of it. And why should death be any different?
Maybe people watching just can't hear the screams.
  I don't know.
  I'm scared and I don't want to die, I don't want to die.
  It's only the thought of you that keeps me sane, Future
Self.

*During this break, Sophie stays, motionless. Daphne,
Judy and Calliope cross the space in front of her,
clearing the stage of everything. Calliope is the last to
move. She stays gazing at Sophie until the others are
gone, then leaves.*

Sophie Sunday 6th December.

Dear Future Self.

Sometimes it feels like everything that's happened in my whole entire life has just been leading up to the moment I'm going to die, every single second of it. But other times it feels like death's just one more thing.

I'm very scared, Future Self.

I hope, out of everything you might remember, you remember better things than this. Because I want you to remember me, to know who I am, but you're going to have the whole of your life to live, too. That's what the Indian boy decided, in the end, in the documentary. He went to his own grave and he cried and then he kissed the woman who was and wasn't his wife and hugged the kids who were and weren't his children and said at least he'd found them so he could say goodbye. It sounds kind of corny when you tell it like that but when you watch it it's the saddest thing ever.

I wonder if you'll watch the film? If you'll come across it late on TV or in the bargain basement of a Blockbuster and start watching it, for no reason, and have a weird sense of, you've seen it before? I wonder who you'll be and what you'll be like. Calliope says we turn to dust and nothing else and Daphne says we go to Jesus and God in Heaven and Judy says that energy never dies, only changes, wind and water and stars. But I reckon we come back. Maybe we don't remember or maybe we choose not to remember but I reckon we all get thousands of lives to live, millions, and only when you've done literally everything there is to do and experienced everything there is to know is there an ending, and there can never be an ending because infinity's infinite.

Wherever you are, Future Self, and whoever you turn out to be, I hope you're happy. I hope you live to a ripe old age and die peacefully in bed surrounded by lots and lots of children and grandchildren and great-grandchildren.

I hope you travel the world and have loads of sex and fall madly in love with people who love you madly back and never regret anything. And I reckon you'll get all of that because karma's got to be on your side, right?

And if you do come looking, and find me – here I am. Maybe you'll be nine or ten, like the Indian boy, in which case Daphne might still be here, and Cal, though who knows about Judy. Or maybe you'll be ninety, and searching for me will be something that's tugged at the edges of your mind for as long as you can remember. Well, if Daphne and Judy and Calliope are still here, tell them we love them, because we do, even Calliope, even though we hate her sometimes, too.

That's all, I think. There's no good place to stop, so it might as well be here.

I'm going to go downstairs now, and I'm going to creep softly so no one will hear me, because if any of them does I know they'll stop me. They'll say I need to conserve my energy, that if I lie still and keep calm the latest transfusion will last for three, four days instead of forty-eight or twenty-four hours. But I don't want to dribble away the last of my precious energy lying in bed. Judy says I'm lucky to have seen all the countries I've seen, but even if I'd been to all the countries in the world twice over it still wouldn't be enough. I'm going to go outside, to the swings, and I'm going to use the rest of my energy to push myself off, and I'm going to swing and swing, higher and higher, swishing through the cold and the sun like I'm faster and sleeker than light.

That's how I want you to think of me, Future Self. OK. Goodbye.

The lights fade slowly.
Then sudden blackout.